To Louise

with best wishes

Anita

28-6-10

TAILORS ON BOTH SIDES

TAILORS ON BOTH SIDES

Anita Canter

First published by Tollington Press, London, 2010
www.tollingtonpress.co.uk

A catalogue record for this book is available from the British Library.

ISBN 978-0-9560173-4-5

Cover photograph: the author's aunt, Poula, and father, Herman

Cover design by Sarah Wood
Typeset by Helen Sandler

Printed in Great Britain by the MPG Books Group, Bodmin and King's Lynn

*For my parents, Jennie and Herman, who gave me life so I could tell this story
to my children and grandchildren*

CONTENTS

1
THE JOSEFSONS

My grandparents, Morfar and Mormor, Landskrona

1 The Josefsons

My two families of origin were very different – one was Danish and the other Swedish – but they had one thing in common: they were both tailors.

My Swedish family had come from Lithuania. My mother's parents, Rosa (*née* Crown) and Jacob Katz, were both born in Vilna, but like so many young Jewish people of that generation, they fled pogroms and persecution to seek a better life elsewhere. They first went to England in the year 1900, to Leeds, where Jacob's cousins, Ray and Bessie Kantor, had already settled. Leeds was the centre of the clothing industry and, both being tailors, they hoped to make a living there.

Their eldest son, Herman, was born in Leeds in 1902, but the smoke, fog and damp weather soon drove them away, and for some reason they went to the small town of Landskrona in Sweden. There they changed their name to Josefson to fit in with Swedish society. Although they did return to Leeds for a period of time, they packed up again when their bank collapsed and went back to Landskrona, where they stayed for good. Two more children came along, Henning in 1904 and Isak in 1907.

I only knew my grandparents as 'old people', who never seemed to want to go anywhere at all, and I could not imagine them to-ing and fro-ing from England to Sweden. The story goes that when they first arrived in Sweden they bought a goat and some chickens to keep in the back yard, as they used to in their small Jewish village (*shtetl*) in Vilna, but it didn't go down very well with their Swedish neighbours, who complained about being woken up so early in the mornings by the noise.

My grandparents, whom I called Morfar and Mormor, started a men's clothing shop called 'Josefson's Herrekipering', which sold suits and men's clothes in general. In the beginning they both worked in the shop, and even later when my grandmother was busy with the fast growing family, she was always consulted when new material had to be purchased and decisions about the business were made.

Apart from working in the shop, my grandfather travelled around the area into the countryside selling his suits and other goods to the local population. He was a socialist all his life, believing that if the workers got more money, they would be able to buy more clothes in his shop! The shop did well, and they gradually rose up to the comfortable middle classes, buying a new car and eventually moving to a spacious modern flat with a balcony.

Two daughters were born: Cecilia in 1910 and, three years later on 13 December 1913, my mother Jennie. She was without doubt the favourite in the family, loved and adored by her parents and brothers, while Cecilia unfortunately became the Cinderella, bossed about by her brothers and, being the eldest girl, given the role of helping with the housework. Josef arrived in 1916, and the baby of the family was Martin, born in 1920 – all in all, seven children.

The Josefsons were well respected by the non-Jewish and Jewish communities in Landskrona, and my grandfather was one of the leaders in the small synagogue. They were orthodox in every sense of the word. They kept strictly kosher, my grandfather prayed and laid *tefillin* every morning, and Saturday (Shabbat) was a true day of rest.

My grandmother was deeply religious. She prayed a lot at home, especially on Shabbat, and read Hebrew and Yiddish religious books. She was very learned and much respected by her husband and children. My grandfather may have been the king in the household – he laid down the law – but everyone knew deep down that Raisel had the last word.

Clothes were important in the Josefson family: being tailors and running a clothes shop, you had to look respectable. It was a big household, but as they became quite comfortable financially, they could afford to look good. They would always comment on what you were wearing, the quality and style of your outfit, and how it looked on you.

There were many remnants of various materials from the shop, and I remember my mother's thrill when she was given some material to bring back to Denmark to be made into dresses, skirts and suits for her and me – and trousers, jackets and coats for my brother, Bent.

There were serious toll restrictions from Sweden to Denmark during those years, and the material had to be sewn into the lining of our clothes in order to smuggle it over the border. My father was an expert in these matters, and I was aware of his excitement in performing those activities. His War experiences came to good use and he seemed to enjoy the challenge. It was not only material that was smuggled across the border – it was also forbidden to bring certain foods into Denmark.

I recall endless visits to the seamstress, Fru Dahl, in Vanløse, Copenhagen. She lived in the next block of flats on the third floor. She had been married to a painter, and her flat was full of wonderful paintings, on the walls and stacked on the floor.

My grandfather was a Zionist, and after the creation of the State of Israel in 1948, he used to sit for hours listening to the radio, trying to catch the broadcasting from over there. There was great joy when he heard the Hebrew words '*Kol Israel*' ('The voice of Israel') and we all had to gather round the radio as if a miracle had just happened.

Like so many Jews of that generation he never went to Israel, but he followed the development of the new state with great enthusiasm. The blue and white money-box, *Keren Kayemet*, was always there in the home. Even before the State of Israel was created, Jewish people collected money in the hope of one day having a country they could call their own.

My grandmother, Raisel, never turned a beggar away – this must have gone round the little town of Landskrona, because beggars frequently knocked on their door. Once, when I opened the door and quickly closed it again without giving any money, my mormor made me run after the beggar to give him a few coins.

Yiddish was the language spoken in the home. Their children understood Yiddish, but answered in Swedish. My grandfather learned Swedish and could read Swedish newspapers, and he was able to conduct all his business in Swedish and understand the news from the radio. My grandmother mostly learned the Swedish she would use for shopping and conversing with customers and neighbours. On the other hand, she was very literate in Hebrew and Yiddish.

Family and friends often visited their home, and during the War (in which Sweden was neutral) and for years afterwards, Jewish survivors of the Holocaust who had found refuge in Landskrona were frequent visitors.

One of them, Magda, a young woman from Czechoslovakia, who had lost all her family in the concentration camps, came to live with my grandparents for a time. She helped in the house, and she was a fantastic acrobat. She used to perform for us children, and she always seemed happy and jolly.

I wonder now what terrible traumas she must have suffered in the camps from losing all her family, but in those days people believed that the less you talked about these painful matters, the better for the person (and for others). Eventually she was given a *shiddach* (an arranged marriage) to a much older man, a rabbi in Czechoslovakia, and she sent us photos of herself and her two beautiful daughters.

To us children, the Josefsons seemed to have an open house to the whole of the Jewish community in Landskrona. Tea, biscuits and cakes were served, and the conversations and discussions in Yiddish and Swedish were loud and lively. At such gatherings the atmosphere was high, filled with good humour, jokes and stories.

Some evenings were very special, almost electric, and when I watched my mother's face, I just knew she was very happy. She was with her parents, whom she loved and idealised, and some of her siblings, who adored her. Such moments were among the happiest in my life.

During those evenings it was a real treat when my grandmother could be persuaded to tell one of her Yiddish stories. It only happened after much urging and begging. Although I understood some Yiddish, I could never quite get the last bit of the story (often the whole point of it), and I had to ask my mother to translate.

I didn't really have proper conversations with my grandparents – more like questions and answers. I was in awe of them, which mainly stemmed from my mother and her siblings' adoration of them. They were very controlling as parents and took many decisions for their children, in some cases going so far as to decide whom they should marry and what type of work they should do. All the sons ended up working in the clothing industry in one way or another.

My admiration for my grandmother got a knock one day, when (at ten years old) I asked her some questions from the Bible. I had asked my mother, and she suggested I should ask Mormor, believing without doubt that she would be able to give me all the 'true' answers. But when I asked her how this or that from the Bible could be possible, she said I should not ask so many questions, I should just believe. From that moment on I decided to make up my own mind regarding these matters – and that you definitely could not rely on the adults to give you proper explanations.

We went to stay with my grandparents in Sweden once a month. Sometimes in summer my mother, Bent and I took a 90-minute ferry trip direct from Copenhagen on the Friday, and my father joined us on the Saturday. In the winter we had to take the train from Copenhagen to Helsingør, then go by boat to Helsingborg where my uncle Jos always came to pick us up in his car. I can still see him standing there waving with a big smile on his face, ready with his jokes.

We arrived just in time for Shabbat and the special Friday night dinner. The candles were lit, my grandmother had baked the traditional plaited bread, challah, and there was a small challah for each of us children. The sweet raisin wine was homemade, and I can still hear my grandmother saying in Yiddish to my mother, 'Let them have some more wine, it will not do them any harm.'

My cousin Esther, who was two years older than me, was often in Landskrona. Her mother Cecilia had a difficult life. She was divorced, and she and Esther lived in a tiny flat in Copenhagen. To me it seemed such a cosy little flat, but obviously not easy for the two of them in such a confined space.

Bent, Esther and I played well together and had great fun, especially at bedtime when we had to share two beds. Who was going to be piggy in the middle?

As the youngest child in Landskrona, Bent got a lot of attention – and he was adored by my mother. I always knew she had a special, close relationship with him and I did not mind too much. I loved him myself intensely; we had always been very close. He being three years younger, I looked after him and protected him and, if anybody did anything to him, I was there with my fists ready to fight them.

During the holidays we would spend a week or more in Landskrona. Esther, who could speak both Swedish and Yiddish, spent many of her holidays there and was very close to my grandmother. We used to play in some of the wonderful parks in Landskrona, where we built dens, and in the summer we went to the seaside and had picnics on the beach at Barsebæk.

My mother was very close to her brother Jos. He married late so, when we were young, he was still living at home. He worked in the shop and gradually took over the business as my grandfather was getting older. He was a wonderful uncle. He was always making fun and he just had to enter a room and people started smiling. No-one could make my father laugh or smile as Jos could. In fact, I was amazed to see my father laugh so loud, even when he had been in one of his many bad moods.

We children used to put pins in Jos's bed and cushions over his head when he was taking his after-lunch nap. He would pretend he didn't notice, then after a while get up with a loud noise and chase us around the flat.

Jos was very musical and my mother would often tell me, with great pride, that he was never taught music, but he could play any tune on the piano and sing beautiful songs. When we were in bed, he used to come in and dance and clown for us. Later my grandmother would come in with homemade biscuits.

Jos was a handsome man with straight black hair and smiling, brown/green eyes, very like my mother's. He was a real charmer and very emotional. To me it seemed he was always either laughing or crying (a common Josefson characteristic).

In later years when he was in hospital for an operation, he and the patient in the next bed got into fits of laughter the night before. They were cracking jokes – mostly 'sick' jokes – about the serious operation. The whole ward was joining in, including nurses and doctors. When he left the hospital, patients and staff were all leaning out of the windows waving goodbye to him.

He loved Yiddish songs, and my father gave him many records and tapes. Even on his deathbed, he could not refrain from joking.

Jos was not without girlfriends, but 'the right one' would have to be from a respectable Jewish family. In 1955 he married Ingrid Rock. They met in Copenhagen, and my mother was involved in the arrangement! Jos and Ingrid spent some days in Copenhagen; they visited us and we all went on a few outings together. She was approved of, and the marriage was quickly arranged in Malmø. The couple had two sons: Ulf was born in 1956 and Rolf in 1957.

Jos seemed to be the only one who was 'allowed' to make fun of his parents and tease them. They just used to shake their heads and accept his, at times, childlike behaviour.

Most of the time my grandfather was very serious and strict. Every time we came to Landskrona, Bent and I had to read from the Hebrew prayer book, so he could monitor our progress. The reward was a little mint pastel from a small box he carried in his waistcoat pocket and some money to buy a little toy in Epa, the local store.

I nearly always bought a little doll, and I remember the thrill of making dolls' clothes and forming a bed for her out of a matchbox. Even the doll had to wear nice clothes.

When we went for a walk in the park my mother often pointed to a tree against which my grandmother had banged her head repeatedly when she first received the news that we had been captured by the Nazis.

The Holocaust was always with us (or at least, with me) as a shadow following us. It would suddenly appear in the adults' conversation, in the expression on their faces, and they would begin to cry. I felt terrified at such a moment; there was nothing I could do to make it better.

The Yiddish culture was entrenched in the family – especially the old songs. When we first got a record player in the late 1940s, my father bought Yiddishe records in Copenhagen, and we played them while we were on the phone to my grandparents in Sweden. Whenever they heard the song 'My Yiddishe Mama', they were all in tears. Such a sentimental and emotional family.

Herman, the eldest son, married an English woman from Leeds, Celia, and they lived in Landskrona for nine years with their son Cecil. He was the first and only grandchild for many years and only five years younger than Martin (his uncle).

He was totally in love with his early childhood in Landskrona, and he had seven adoring aunts and uncles – of whom my mother was a special favourite. In later life, he remembered often sitting on my grandmother's lap, while she told him stories of her childhood in Lithuania. One of the stories was that her parents were like Gypsies and used to travel round in a caravan selling pots and pans.

When Cecil was nine the family was 'strongly encouraged' by my grandfather to move to Copenhagen, so Cecil could be sure to go to the Jewish School and get a proper Jewish education. Cecil had a sister called Irene Solveig, but she died as a very young child.

Herman died during the War, in 1942, of TB – never to see his second son, Flemming, being born. After the War Celia took the children to live in Los Angeles in the USA (near Hollywood). She married again (*shiddach*), and they sent us photos of sunshine and swimming pools.

Cecil married Audrey from Leeds. They had one son, Peter. Cecil kept in touch with the family, and regularly visited relatives in Copenhagen, Leeds, Liverpool and Landskrona. Cecil was very much a Josefson like his uncle Jos – the same mad humour, the same charm – they were like brothers.

The Josefsons had a real problem with separation. They cried when we arrived, and they cried when we left. They even cried when they spoke to each other on the phone.

The funerals were a nightmare; so utterly different from the very stiff and formal Swedish protocol. The Josefsons cried loud and shouted, and they gave long speeches to the dead. For a young person it was too much to bear. Esther and I used to cling to each other with fear.

Jos was the uncle we were closest to, because he had been single and lived with our grandparents for such a long time. However, in 1952, my mother's youngest brother, Martin, came to live in Landskrona with his beautiful wife Margot. Martin had been ill with TB – I remember clearly my mother being heartbroken when the news reached us – but he survived, and my grandfather offered him a job in the shop. They had a little girl, three years old, called Rita. Now there was another family to visit in Landskrona, and Margot loved welcoming visitors into her home. She was very warm and charming. Another two children came along: Anikka in 1954 and Thord in 1958.

Martin was more serious than Jos, and spiritually he was very religious. The religion meant a lot to him, and he was the one who remained most observant. He was warm and affectionate, very sincere and, like all the Josefsons, knew how to talk to people.

There was a little competition between the two families: who should we visit when we came to Landskrona? My mother got on well with both her sisters-in-law; and after her death, my father had a real soft spot for Martin and his son Thord.

We did not see much of my other uncles, Henning and Isak, because they lived in Göteborg, but when we did see them, especially Henning, we felt so much love and warmth. He had the same charm as the others, and after my mother's death, he and his wife Bertha invited me to Göteborg where he told me with great emotion many stories about my mother. I always wondered why they had not seen more of each other.

In the early days, when my grandparents were alive, the religion played a very big part. I remember standing on the balcony on Saturday evening with my grandmother trying to find three stars. That meant Shabbat was over, and that we could put the lights on. We said Havdala, with Bent holding the candle up high (while Jos was tickling him) and we welcomed the new week with the overflowing cup of wine and smelling the spices.

Bent, Esther and I had to attend synagogue on Shabbat and on Jewish festivals. On Simchat Torah we marched around waving the Israeli flag and we got a bag full of sweets. The rabbi, Mr Block, was rather formidable and, like my grandfather, he always wanted to test our Hebrew knowledge. I remember trying to avoid him. One

Shabbat, though, my mother and I met him in the park. As he was talking to my mother, I drew some lines on the stony path with my shoe. I was told off; this was strictly forbidden on the Sabbath. I remember my mother's embarrassment.

On the Sunday before we travelled back to Copenhagen, we often went out in the car to the Saxtorp forest. Two deckchairs were brought, so my grandparents could sit and smell the fresh air and the fir trees. Photos were taken and then home to coffee and cakes. The countryside was not really part of their lives, and certainly not for spending much time in – long walks were out of the question. Later, when my uncles bought small summerhouses in the country, my grandfather could not see the purpose. He said: 'What do you think we are, cows?'

We all felt an affinity to the Gypsies; they were dark like us, they looked a bit like us, and Jos, especially, liked to visit them in their caravans. There were several Gypsy camps on the outskirts of Landskrona, and Jos used to tease me that they wanted a dark girl like me. Once I hid in our car – I believed him.

At big celebrations and social gatherings the Josefsons really came into their own. I especially remember my grandparents' Golden Wedding in 1950. Everybody was there: Henning and Bertha with son Bertil, Martin and Margot, Isak and Jenny and son Lennart. Jos was there sitting in the middle of his parents and the five grandchildren at the front of the picture. Our two boy cousins were two years older than me, and it was a real treat for Bent, Esther and me to play with them.

The party was held at home in Regeringsgatan 53, and a long table was laid for family and friends. The speeches were plentiful and very emotional. My grandparents were praised to the hilt. After the meal it was time for self-entertainment, and many of the older generation sang these wonderful Yiddish songs. The whole place seemed to be buzzing. Even my brother, who was six at the time and toothless, sang 'Rudolph the Red-Nosed Reindeer' – not exactly a fitting song for a Jewish party, but everybody enjoyed it.

Even as a child I appreciated these wonderful moments with this family, the richness of the culture, the warmth and togetherness of it all, and I just felt so lucky. I remember a special moment as a 16-year-old leaning up against the wall in my grandparents' flat thinking: How long can this go on; how long will all my family still be alive like now?

How is it possible to write an ending and a summary of these years, when I didn't want it to end at all? There is a Yiddish song which is always on my mind when I think back to those years:

Oh how can we bring back those years, Moishele my friend?
Oh those long forgotten wonderful years.

Top: My grandfather's shop: Herman, Morfar and Henning, Landskrona
Above: My grandparents' Golden Wedding with all the cousins in front: Bertil, Anita, Lennart, Esther and Bent, Landskrona, 1950
Left: My father, mother, Jos, Ingrid, Bent, with Anita and Esther behind, Køge, Denmark, 1954

My mormor's parents, my great-grandparents, Vilna; my grandparents, Mormor and Morfar, with Isak, Herman, Cecilia and Henning

All the Josefsons – Cecil on Henning's knee, Landskrona; my grandmother in the kitchen in Landskrona

Jos, Landskrona; Magda with her daughters, Chaja and Chava, Grenoble, 1951

My mother Jennie and her sister Cecilia; Anita and Esther

This page, from top: Esther, Jos, Bent and Anita, Vanløse, Copenhagen; Regeringsgatan 53, Landskrona, with my grandparents' balcony marked; (left to right) Bent, Jos, my father, Mormor, Morfar, my mother and myself

Opposite, from top: Anita, Bent and Esther at Simchat Torah; a trip to the forest: Anita, my mother, Bent, Esther, Mormor and Morfar, Landskrona; Jos, Morfar, Mormor, Jennie, Martin, Landskrona, 1955

2
THE SVERDLINS

My grandparents, Farmor and Farfar, Copenhagen

2 The Sverdlins

It was said that the Sverdlins were one of the most unusual and beautiful looking families in Copenhagen.

My grandfather was very dark and attractive, and my grandmother had big blue eyes with sad, heavy eyelids and dark skin. Their children were all dark with thick, black, curly hair, except Max, who had golden curls. They were Ashkenazis, coming from Eastern Europe, but they could easily have originated from Spain, Turkey, Africa or India, as the Sephardi Jews did.

My father's parents – my *farmor* and *farfar*, as I called them – each came from Russia to Denmark around 1909. My grandfather, Michel Teveler Sverdlin, was born in Polotyk near Vitebsk on 4 May 1889. His father was Torio Sverdlin, a carpenter, and his mother was Minje, *née* Aluf. Michel fled Russia to avoid being conscripted into the Russian Army for a duration of 20 years. This law meant that you most certainly would not see your sons again. It was just another example of anti-Semitism, which was rampant in Russia and Eastern Europe. Michel and his brother, Aron Salman (Samke), arrived in Copenhagen in 1909; their parents, one brother and one sister remained in Vitebsk.

My grandmother, Mariassa Minkov, was born on 15 August 1892 in Minsk. She was the daughter of Hirsh Minkov and Pesche, *née* Grasnik. They had eleven children but only six of them survived. My grandmother was number six. Hirsh bought goods like corn and flour from the nearby farmer and then sold them to other people. They lived at the end of town and were very poor. They never knew if they had enough to go around… every day was a struggle. Hirsh died in 1897 and Pesche married again, but the second marriage was not happy and they later divorced.

Mariasse and her sister Dobe left Minsk after their mother's death in 1910 and travelled to Copenhagen to join their older brother Boris and sister Bracha. (Boris married Manja and they had two daughters, Poula and Fanny; Bracha married Matesof and had five children.)

Then two brothers married two sisters: Michel married Mariasse and Samke married Dobe.

All the men in the family were tailors of some kind, but their expertise varied from cutting materials to sewing suits, waistcoats, dresses and coats – or making button holes. The Sverdlins were not Zionists like the Josefsons; their background was in the Yiddish-speaking Socialist movement known as the Bund, formed in 1897. The only politically active member of the family, though, was Samke. To my grandparents' great embarrassment, he was a Communist, and he collected money for the Jewish area or state in Russia called Birobidijan.

My grandmother did not like to talk about her childhood in Russia. She never went to school and never learnt to read or write. She worked for a time in a matchstick factory. She remembered hiding in the cellars during the Easter period, which was the traditional time for anti-Semitic riots, and she was often spat at and called names. She also remembered being called a Gypsy, which seemed to be an added insult, and when she came to Denmark she just couldn't believe that she could walk down the street and nobody would call her names; it was like arriving in paradise.

My father, Hirsh Herman, was the eldest child, born on 29 September 1913; and less than two years later, on 1 May 1915, came Pesche Poula (known as Poula). That same year, on 28 November 1915, Samke and Dobe were married, and my grandparents organised the wedding party for them in their flat on the second floor of Rosengarden 5. The invitation was in both Danish and Yiddish, and the ceremony was to take place in Ny Kongensgade 6 at six o'clock.

During those days the expectations were not high; people were just grateful and pleased that they would be able to celebrate a wedding in small and modest conditions – and most importantly in an atmosphere devoid of fear of ridicule or persecution.

Four years later on 10 July 1919 another little daughter was born. She was given the name Mery Vera (and known as Vera). Both parents worked day and night to make ends meet, and they now felt that their family was complete. However, six years later it came as a great shock to my grandmother when she found she was pregnant again. She told me that she went to the doctor feeling extremely depressed, she just did not know how she would be able to cope. The doctor remarked that perhaps this child would be a special blessing to her, and as it turned out, Max, born on 16 February 1925, grew up to be a gentle and thoughtful boy who was always very caring and loving toward his mother. When Oscar arrived two years later on 21 December 1926, my grandmother just accepted her fate, and he became the baby of the family.

Poula, the eldest daughter, was soon helping with the sewing. From the age of ten she was taught how to cut and sew material, and she developed into a very competent seamstress and later became a superb tailor. When I grew up she made some of my clothes, and no-one knew better how to get it just right.

Clothes were to become very important in the Sverdlin family, and all the children were beautifully dressed in the latest fashions with all kinds of details on their dresses and suits. This became the hallmark for the family, and as with the Josefsons in Sweden, it was always noticed what you were wearing and how it suited you.

In 1925 my grandfather's parents, Torio and Minje Sverdlin from Vitebsk, came to stay with them for several months. It was a wonderful, emotional reunion for them as they had not seen their two sons for 16 years and were meeting their daughters-in-law and several grandchildren for the first time. Their flat was only small, but in those days people were used to cramped conditions. For Vera, who was six at the time, this period seems very vivid: her grandmother in her long black skirt, and sitting with her grandfather on some steps opposite the house eating an apple.

At the end of their visit they applied for asylum; they desperately wanted to stay in Denmark, but regrettably their application was refused. Vera remembers the heartbreaking tragedy, when they had to say goodbye, knowing they would never see each other again.

The Sverdlins were not religious or observant, but they kept a kosher home and celebrated the festivals with traditional food. My father went to the Jewish school for boys, and Poula and Vera went to the Jewish girls' school. Max and Oscar attended the local school, and when it was time for their Barmitzvah, they had private lessons in Hebrew.

My grandparents spoke Yiddish at home, and the children understood, but answered in Danish. When my father was old enough to play in the streets, he taught his Danish playmates Yiddish.

My grandfather was a quiet and gentle man. He learned both reading and writing in Danish, although not to a very high standard; but my grandmother never learned to read or write in Danish. She learned to speak Danish, but she always had a strong accent. She never missed the news though: the radio was tuned to Radio Avis every hour, a habit that stayed with the family for years. Danger was always round the corner – you never knew when, but you had to be prepared.

The Sverdlins were not as noisy or outgoing as the Josefsons, but they were warm and affectionate and always interested in you as a person – often hugging and kissing you. My father, as the eldest son, was looked up to and spoiled. He took the role of looking after the family very seriously. He quickly learned to speak Danish better than his parents, and they had to turn to him when they got letters from the authorities, or messages they could not understand.

He became very protective and responsible, but at times dominant, especially toward his sisters. He took it as his task to look after them. They were a little frightened of him and had much more respect for him than for their own father. When they started going out with boys, he used to follow them to see what they were up to, and if he did not approve of their choice of boyfriend, he told them off. He was the only one who had his own bedroom; the others had to share. Max and Oscar had to sleep on put-up beds in the living room, the girls had to sleep in the workroom among the cloths, sewing machines and irons, but my father had his room all to himself. When he was taking a nap during the day, they all had to tiptoe in case they woke him up.

My aunt Poula had her hands full. Not only did she help with the sewing, but she was also in charge of her two younger brothers, and she had to push them in the pram to the park. She was very proud of them, because people used to stop and admire those two handsome little boys with their long curly hair: Max's was golden and Oscar's was black.

Vera was an unusual and special beauty, and the story goes that she always had a headache when there were jobs to be done in the house like helping with the washing up. One job she did perform, though, was taking my grandfather's beautiful golden pocket watch to the pawn shop when there was no money in the kitty – and retrieving it again when my grandparents got paid by the consumers. There are several marks on the pocket watch to prove it, made in the shop.

Poula and Vera were both so beautiful. I used to be very proud of my two aunts with their thick black hair done up in lovely hairstyles. They preferred straight hair, and when they were young they used an iron to make it straight. I loved to hear stories from their childhood and youth.

The Sverdlins were a solid, respectable family, and it came as a shock when they discovered that my grandparents had not been legally married when their children were born. The wedding ceremony was led by Chief Rabbi Dr. Friediger on 8 May 1928 and the witnesses were Ruben Cress (tailor) and Leibe Bekjakof (businessman).

For the Sverdlins it was of utmost importance that the boys should get a proper trade, so they could earn their own living. My father became a furrier, Max a printer and Oscar an electrician. As was usual then, the girls were not expected to get 'proper' qualifications but, as it turned out, Poula became a superb seamstress and Vera worked in a factory for a time and lost half her thumb, later working with her husband Ernest in their paper factory.

Poula married Knud, a non-Jew, who later converted to Judaism, taking a new middle name to become Knud David Larsen. He always had a twinkle in his eyes, and he loved Yiddish expressions. He was an only child and came from a very Danish working-class background. They had one beautiful daughter called Nina; she was the 'apple of their eye' and could have been a model.

Vera married Ernest Isacksen, whose parents came from Norway. He had a twin sister called Tutte, who was very beautiful with flaming red hair. Ernest himself had red hair and masses of freckles. He also had an older brother called Rudolf.

Vera and Ernest's wedding took place in Malmø during the War, and my parents made their wedding party – something Ernest never forgot. He had to mention it in all his speeches with great emotion at every family celebration.

How lucky I was to have such wonderful uncles on both sides of the family – these thoughts often crossed my mind – and I did appreciate it.

Ernest loved a good argument and a lively discussion. He often took the opposite view just to get things going. We discussed politics and religion especially, and from an early age I happily joined in, loving every minute of it. I learned to express my opinions, and I found it stimulating and interesting to think about those subjects.

Vera and Ernest had two sons, Alf and Arne – some years younger than Bent and me – and we always got on well with our cousins, whom we saw regularly at birthday celebrations and family gatherings.

My grandfather died at the age of 56 in 1947. He suffered a great deal from the War experience. My grandmother was so sad, and I was aware of her sadness. Being the eldest grandchild I held a special position, and I knew I was very much loved. I used to stroke her soft cheeks and play with her golden earrings, while she called me affectionate Yiddish names.

Max and Oscar were wonderful uncles, only 14 and 16 years older than me. They lived with my grandmother, and we saw them often. They played games with Bent and me and bought us a white mouse and two canaries. They were so loving and so full of fun.

Oscar lived with my grandmother until she died in 1960. She was the grandparent I was closest to; she looked after me when my mother was in hospital in Malmø giving birth to Bent, and she survived my mother by two years. She was heartbroken to witness my father's despair, and wished she had died instead of my mother. She often had us for dinner at the Jewish festivals – and she tried hard to look after us the best she could. Her mother had died when she was a young girl, so she knew what it was like. I think of her often, and I still feel very close to her. Somehow I sense her presence around and it fills me with warmth and love.

Oscar was like a brother to me and helped me through some difficult times, especially when I had big rows with my father after my mother's death. Once in the middle of the night after such a row, I walked out and took the train and bus up to Oscar's summerhouse. I did not need to say much; Oscar understood and quickly went to the nearest telephone booth to tell my father where I was.

When my father was against me going to teacher training college, Oscar gave me money to buy books. My father believed I did not need professional qualifications

– I should 'only get married'! Oscar was a wonderful support in those days, but he never said anything against my father; none of the family did. They had always been a little frightened of him, and now they felt so sorry for him, losing my mother and being so lonely. In their eyes he was the one who had suffered, and he needed support. Bent and I had to fit in.

For me to leave Denmark and live in England was a real problem for the Sverdlin family. I was told my place was to stay at home and look after my father and brother! That created terrible conflicts within me, displeasing my wonderful family, but in the end I had to do it – it felt like survival. But fifty years ago, the expectations for a girl were different. All this became clear when I entered the Women's Movement in the early 1970s – such joy and solidarity listening to other women's lives – you did not feel so alone. Perhaps it was also my mother's voice from 'above', and remembering her talking about women's emancipation.

As it turned out, it was all resolved later and the Liverpool family connection added an extra dimension to the Sverdlins – and most important, the closeness in the family was sustained.

Max left Copenhagen in 1953 to live in Assens and later in Ålborg to set up his own printing business. At that stage nobody knew he was secretly living with Tina, a maid at Hertz Printing Works, where he was an apprentice. Tina was twenty years older than him, and after the War they renewed their relationship, finally marrying in Ålborg. The whole family was in shock.

I will never forget the evening when we were going to meet Tina for the first time. She was not Jewish, which was very difficult for my grandmother and my father. I had been aware of the controversy going on in the family through my mother. For her, it was no problem – I even felt some of her excitement regarding the new development – but my father was in one of his many terrible moods.

On the way to my grandmother's flat, where the whole family was assembled to meet this new member of the family, my mother told me not to stare at her. This is exactly what I did, and I was fascinated by this sweet woman, to whom the evening must have been like a trial. She was warmly welcomed by my mother, aunts and uncles, who took to her straight away.

Max and Tina never had any children, and she sadly died fairly young. Max took everybody by surprise again, this time marrying a woman twenty years younger than himself, Vibeke, and they had two children, Michael and Maj-brit.

Oscar never married, and we used to rent a summerhouse each year together with him and my grandmother. To Bent and me these holidays were wonderful; Oscar used to play with us, and I did not have to help with the housework – not that I ever did much of that anyway.

There was a very distinct immature streak in the Sverdlins, and they could easily get into fits of laughter. Their humour was childish but catching; outsiders just used to shake their heads, as if they were dealing with *meshuggeners* (mad people). Oscar at times could not contain himself and had to leave the room – usually over a silly joke.

Poula was even worse. When she was sewing for me and had to put pins in the material, the pins sometimes pricked me – that was it, she could hardly stop herself laughing – or if she saw somebody tripping over something – to her that was very funny.

No-one loved the sun and summers as much as the Sverdlins. At the first beam of sunlight, they were all out anywhere to enjoy it. It could be on their balcony or in the park nearby, and they all rented somewhere in the country, if only a few rooms, so they could spend time outside in the sun. You needed that after the Danish winters which were usually very cold. I can still see the lines of sun-worshippers lying on the grass or on the sunbeds and deckchairs in Oscar's garden. He bought a summerhouse with a big garden in 1957, where the whole family assembled during the weekends, enjoying the sunshine and swimming in Øresund. They all brought their own food, and Oscar served tea, coffee and cakes.

We had several trips to the kiosks just down the road to buy ice-creams. The next generation – my children, Jan and Nina, Bent's son, Rami, and my cousins' children, also enjoyed many happy hours in Oscar's garden. Even the next generation, my grandchildren, if only the older ones, remember playing there with Oscar's toys and receiving small presents and sweets. Later each family bought their own little summerhouse (*kolonihave*) and the family was more split.

In the early days everybody's birthday was celebrated in great style – something the Danes are very good at. The table was laid with homemade cakes and biscuits – and most importantly, a large birthday cake. My mother's sister Cecilia would be there with my cousin Esther and we would all sing 'Happy Birthday' in both Danish and Swedish.

As a child I was not aware of any negative undercurrents in the family and I seldom heard my parents talking badly about anybody. When I looked around the table, I saw smiling faces – at times teasing and joking with each other, but with love and good humour. We were all very close in those days, and I felt so lucky belonging to this warm and affectionate family.

Reflections

I used to have debates with myself about which family I felt closest to. When I travelled back from Sweden, I was glad to get home to the Sverdlins – to their warmth, practical solidarity and dependable ways; and when I was in Denmark, I could not wait to see my Swedish family – the outgoing, slightly 'mad' and noisy Josefsons.

Within our own little family, there was some sort of divide. My father and I were the Danes, both born in Denmark – and my mother and Bent were the Swedes. During a football match between Denmark and Sweden, which we always listened to on the radio, we knew who to support.

I know I have taken from both families. I have within me both Sverdlin and Josefson. The importance that was attached to clothes, I got from both families – a double dosage. No wonder I never tire of looking round the shops. When everyone else is flopping, I am still eager to see more.

My great-grandparents

My grandparents, Farmor and Farfar, Copenhagen

Dobbe, Baris, my great-grandmother Pesche and my farmor Mariassa, Minsk; my father, Poula and baby Vera with their parents, Copenhagen

My aunt and father, Poula and Herman, pictured with their namesake cousins and alone

Back row: unknown, Poula, my father, cousin Herman; front row: Vera, cousin Poula and baby Max; Copenhagen

Left to right: Poula, my farmor, my father, Oscar, Max, my farfar and Vera, Copenhagen

Right: Cousin Nina
Below: (front) Farmor,
Arne, Alf, Vera and
(behind) my father,
mother, Bent, myself
and Ernest

Opposite page:
Top left: Vera and Ernest
Top right: Poula and Knud
Bottom: Summers with
Farmor and Oscar

3
MY PARENTS

My parents, Hirsh Herman Sverdlin and Jennie (née Josefson)

3 My Parents

My parents' marriage was a real love match. They met at a party in Copenhagen in 1936. My mother had travelled from Landskrona in Sweden to meet some other young Jewish people – and it was love at first sight.

Three of my mother's siblings were also to settle in Copenhagen: Cecilia with her husband Abraham Markus and their daughter Esther; Herman with his wife Celia from England and their son Cecil; and Henning, married to Bertha, with their son Bertil.

My parents made a very attractive couple; they got engaged on 4 July 1937 and a year later on 3 July 1938 they were married. It was the wedding of the year in Landskrona, and my mother's father, my morfar, lavishly spent a great deal of money to make this occasion an unforgettable event. He and Mormor had no part in arranging the match, but they felt happy about the choice of son-in-law. My father had a steady job as a furrier in one of the biggest fur shops in Copenhagen, and he came from a solid Jewish family.

The Sverdlins loved my mother from the start, and she was happy marrying into this warm and affectionate family. She called her mother-in-law Mrs Sverdlin and was very formal with her. This was the strict Swedish protocol and how you addressed older people in those days.

The holidays we later shared with my farmor and Oscar were often for economic reasons, and even if I detected some reservations from my mother's side, they were never expressed outright. I did, however, pick up the feeling that no woman could ever be as clever and wonderful as her own mother, my mormor.

My mother had a very lively and attractive personality; she was tall and slim like most of her siblings, with twinkly brown/green smiling eyes, and people took to her straight away. She was used to a great deal of attention, which gave her confidence and a certain charm. She knew how to talk to people – as did all the Josefsons. Years later when my uncle, Ernest Isacksen, was starting a new factory, he especially wanted my mother to be present at the opening in order to create a good atmosphere.

I would often lie in bed listening to my mother's voice when they had visitors – usually the family. Bent and I were sent to bed after we had politely shaken hands with everyone (and received hugs and kisses), but we lived in a small flat, and when we were lying in bed, we could hear the conversation through the thin walls. My mother's voice came steadily through, keeping the conversation going, as I imagined it. I hoped one day I would be like her.

My father was very well respected by many people – feared a little by his own family, but loyal, and trusted and admired by his work colleagues. He left school at 15 and began to train as an apprentice in a fur shop. He worked in that shop, Birger Christensen, nearly all his life, except for the three years in Sweden during the War, and he was a very skilled craftsman. He became the foreman for the workshop, and he even trained the owner's son, Finn Christensen. That family was half-Jewish and also had to flee to Sweden during the War. Finn often came to my parents' flat in Malmø and stayed overnight.

After the War Finn took over the running of the shop; he developed it into the most exclusive modern fur shop in Copenhagen – even delivering fur coats to the Danish Royal family. Nina inherited a little white fur coat from the Greek Princess Alexandra.

My father received a medal from the Danish Queen Margrethe II for 50 years' service to the firm; and Finn Christensen used every opportunity to advertise the shop through him. When my father turned 70 and 75, the firm put on big parties for him, and the press was there. He was still working part-time when he died at the age of 75.

He received another medal from the Queen when he had given 50 litres of blood. He had the rare blood group O Rhesus Negative, which was compatible with all blood types, and he was often picked up by an emergency ambulance to give blood during his working hours.

My father liked helping people. He always assisted mothers with prams and toddlers, and he helped people to carry heavy bags. Once when we were all watching a film in the community centre in Liverpool, the film projector broke down. My father quickly offered to help by holding this or that for the projectionist, so he could get on with trying to fix the machine. The rest of the audience did not lift a finger, just complained. Eventually the camera was working again, maybe thanks to my father's encouragement.

Right up to his death, he did the shopping for some of the elderly people in his building, Havekrogen 5, in spite of living on the third floor without a lift.

Just as he could be stern, moody and controlling with his family, he was also loyal and brave, especially when physical pain was at stake. He had all his teeth out in one go with no anaesthetic.

He was totally heartbroken when my mother died. They were both 44 years old.

As he had left most of the communication to her, he was very difficult to get on with. Bent and I had always been a little frightened of him, and now there was no-one to smooth the path for us. Bent and I became even closer; we stuck together and tried to support each other as best we could. My father exhibited terrible moods and tempers, controlling behaviour and unreasonable requests. We were both teenagers trying to be like other young people, but my father found it difficult to relate to us. We were never able to sit down and talk things through.

When I was living in England, I wrote to Bent to sympathise after my father had put him through a particularly difficult time. Unfortunately my father read the letter. He must have been very hurt, but when he referred to it, he just said: 'Let us talk no more about it.'

However, my father made up for all that when he became a grandfather – a farfar to Rami and morfar to my children, Jan and Nina. There was nothing he would not do for them; he was utterly fair and showed no favouritism, loving all three the same. He allowed them to do almost anything – everything his own children were never allowed.

When they were very young, he would sometimes look after them on his own. Being a very practical man, he would cook, clean, wash their clothes and take them to the beach, the zoo, Tivoli and Oscar's summerhouse – while Philip and I had a holiday.

He loved coming to visit his Liverpool family, and he was very popular with all the Canters and friends of the family; he altered their fur coats and made fur animals for the children. To Jan and Nina's friends he was called Morfar. He always got a warm reception in Liverpool's Allerton Synagogue from the Rabbi as the 'visitor from Copenhagen', and he loved that recognition.

Like all the Sverdlins, he had a very childish sense of humour, and some of the stories he told the children are well known today. When he was with his grandchildren, his own child self came out, and he was able to let himself be with them in a way he had not been with his own children.

He came often, alone or with Bent, Rami or Oscar – at times they all came together. He was also very welcoming to our friends from Liverpool who visited Copenhagen. They would stay with him for several nights, and he cooked for them and made sure they knew how to get round Copenhagen: which bus or train to take and where to get off. Nina stayed with my father for two months before she 'made *aliyah*' (moved to Israel), and she worked in one of Birger Christensen's shops. Jan also got work in Copenhagen before he took up his law studies in London. Nothing was too much for my father regarding the family and especially his grandchildren.

When we moved to Israel ourselves in 1986, he was very excited, and he often came to visit. He loved being in Israel. However, there was something very special about his last visit in September 1988. It happened to be his 75th birthday and he wanted to celebrate it with us. We went out for a meal, and Philip's mother Ethel came with us, but sadly his father Sam had passed away three months previously.

My father insisted on staying in a hotel during the last week of his visit, which was most unusual. He was in such great spirits, and Philip and I made a surprise visit to the hotel. That pleased him no end. There was so much unspoken reconciliation during that last visit.

I said goodbye to my father in our lounge in Kfar Saba. We shook hands and embraced. It was a very strange moment. He had planned to come again three months later; in fact I urged him to come, and he showed that letter to Bent and was very moved. But that was never to be. He died a 'happy' man on 4 January 1989 (28 Tevet) doing what he loved doing: cooking a meal for Bent and Rami. He had a major heart attack and died instantly.

My father survived my mother by 31 years. We knew he had several friends, but he always kept them separate from his life with his family. Then, the day after he died, a woman we had never heard of phoned to speak to my father. Bent told her that he had passed away, and she burst out crying. She said she had known him for 29 years.

At the funeral a woman turned up, beautifully dressed in a fur coat and hat, and we embraced near my father's grave. She knew us all from photos, and even asked about Philip's back. We were all amazed. She invited us to her flat, and Bent, Nina and I were stunned, listening to this fantastic story of a relationship which lasted 29 years, which we knew nothing about. My father was the love of her life, his photo being on her bedside table, and she had bought a summerhouse because he enjoyed spending time in the country.

Lovely Lissy Juul, well-dressed and smart looking, a wonderful cook and baker, had spent all those years with my father. He knew all her family, but she was never allowed to know any of his. She knew the rules of the game, it had to be secret, and she loved him very much. In principle my father had always been against this kind of 'mixed liaison' for the family, so how could he now reconcile it for himself?

After his death I was in shock for a long time. It would have lightened things considerably for me, over the years, to have known he had someone who really loved him. Instead he played that lonely man whose wife had died, and he always looked so sad when he waved goodbye to us.

The Sverdlins had a real problem accepting Lissy and the fact that they had been kept in the dark. They thought they were so close. Lissy, Bent and I have been in contact ever since the revelation; we write letters, and she sends me cuttings from

Danish newspapers about Israel or Jewish themes. I visit her every time I am in Copenhagen. When Bent and I asked her how she could put up with my father's prejudices, she said she knew it was that – or nothing at all. Lissy believed that my father had made a pact with God to keep my mother's memory in that manner.

Of my parents, my mother was to have the greatest influence on me. I felt extremely close to her, and loved her very much. In many ways she was my role model. My mother was very Swedish, and she had retained a great deal of the culture and customs. She kept her accent all her life.

The number of Jewish families in Landskrona was small, and although her parents were strictly orthodox, there was no Jewish school, so most of her friends were not Jewish.

I often asked her to tell me stories from when she was little, because I imagined she had been particularly happy during that period. It was a real battle to have my hair washed (I disliked it intensely), so in order to persuade me, she told me incidents from her childhood. There was one story I liked to hear again and again: one Christmas she and some of her siblings secretly bought a Christmas tree, and when they had finished decorating it, the door bell rang. The rabbi, Mr Block, stood outside the door. They quickly put the Christmas tree in the toilet, and hoped he would not need to go in there.

When she was with her girlfriends having fun and being mischievous and they met my grandfather, they all curtsied and said 'good-day Mr Josefson', but he didn't recognise her because he was very short-sighted.

Another story was about a dog they loved dearly, but which was not allowed in their new house. It kept running away and coming back to them.

My mother and her brother Isak were the only children in the family who went to high school. She learned languages and spoke English very well. She later trained as a nurse, but she never completed her training. She also did domestic science for a while, but her great regret in life was that she had no proper professional qualifications. She would have loved to have had a job – to be able to work and earn some money.

She spoke often to me about women who had fought for women's rights, emancipation, women's suffrage, and she was very friendly with a woman nearby who lived with a man without being married. My mother was very conventional and she did not dare to do unconventional things, but she admired the ones who did. She repeatedly instilled in me how important it was for a woman to be able to keep herself, and this was quite often linked to having a good pension and being self-sufficient.

She did take up painting on tiles and porcelain, and she had lessons from a woman who lived in the street, but it felt like a poor substitute for earning your own money and being independent.

I always had the sense that the early years of their marriage were really happy. Photos of my mother showed a radiant looking, beautiful woman.

After the War when we returned from Sweden, the Sverdlin family was very close. Everyone was busy re-establishing their lives again, and my mother was no exception. We all lived in small flats with no cars, and money was scarce, but the security of the closeness in the family made up for lack of funds. I always looked forward to birthdays, when the whole family was together.

My mother's health was not so good. She seemed weak physically, and she had people helping her sometimes when it was wash day. I was terrified when she was not well, but intermittently she seemed to recover, and then everything was fine – until she got ill again.

The summers were always the best: my mother just loved the sunshine, and I can see her in the park on Grøndals Parkvej, just across the road from Havekrogen, lying on a blanket on the grass with her bag full of homemade biscuits or cake, and a Thermos flask of coffee. Her hair was up, and she was wearing a pretty sundress, while Bent played around – with me next to her reading a book.

One summer evening in a rented summerhouse, we all played a game: we had to jump on one leg with an alarm clock to time us, to see who was the fastest. Both my parents were laughing and we had such fun. Such moments were magical – to see my mother happy, letting herself go.

She and I did have our conflicts, and they were nearly always about what clothes I should wear. Whatever she suggested I did not like! She often called me 'envis' in Swedish, meaning stubborn, and she was the only person I dared to be rude to. Once she smacked me on my face, because I was very late home. No wonder she was worried – outside was thunder and lightning. I just burst out laughing, I was so surprised.

I often told her I loved her, and that she was the best mum in the world. She liked to hear that. And I liked to hear the story about when I was born: she wrote to all her brothers that she was the happiest woman in the world.

During her last years she was in and out of hospital, and the medical profession did not know what caused her sickness. When we visited her in hospital, my stomach turned to knots, and it was only a stern warning look from my father which stopped me from crying. My heart sank, and there was nothing I could do.

She died of leukemia on 1 March 1958 (9 Adar). Bent was just 14 and I was 17, and although she had been very ill, we never thought she would die. The two families were in total shock, and she was mourned by so many people. We could not talk about her without crying, so consequently she was not mentioned a lot until years later. When my father spoke to Jos on the telephone, they would both sit holding the telephone receiver for a long time, unable to speak.

Many years later, when Philip, Jan, Nina and I visited my father in Copenhagen, we always made a trip over to Sweden to visit my two uncles and their families in Landskrona. By then they had bought summerhouses, and if we came in the summer, we spent lovely days with them there. They made us feel very welcome.

My uncle Jos died in 1986. Nina was in Israel at the time, and when I told her, she seemed very upset. During the following night Nina had a wonderful dream in which my mother came to her and told her not to be sad, because she and Jos were now together, and they were looking after each other. I felt so moved that my mother, who never met Nina, made a connection with her.

We are all connected in life and in death – nothing separates us – not now, not later – and our soul and spirit will never die.

Reflections

Two important events took place in the last year of my mother's life which both helped me to grow up a little.

I was 16 and had just finished school when my mother and I went for a walk in the park. To my surprise she asked me if I felt I had had a good childhood. I was just about to begin working in the Jewish Kindergarten, and I felt really grown up and important. I reassured her that I'd had a wonderful childhood, and she seemed very pleased.

The second event happened only a month before she died. I was going out on a date and she was not nice to me; she was critical in a manner she had never been before. I was upset, because I knew she must have been feeling bad herself. When I came home there was a little note on my pillow apologising:

'Dear Anita,
I am sorry that I was a little strict with you, but you know I have not been myself these last few weeks. You said yourself that if one is well everything will be fine. Just you see that things will work out for you. I know this for certain. Sleep well, little you, and be as happy and good as you usually are. Your mum'

Bent and I with my mother some months before she died, Vanløse, Copenhagen, 1957

Afterthoughts

Looking back, the years after my mother passed away were not easy. The year before, my maternal grandmother, Mormor, had died, and two years later none of my grandparents were living. I felt as if my whole childhood had gone, and I did not have enough strategies to continue. It took a great deal of loss and grief to work through it all – and endless amounts of counselling sessions.

How blessed and lucky I was to enter the counselling world, in more than one way. Not only for my own healing, but training as a counsellor led me first to re-evaluation, co-counselling, meeting people from all over the world, working on liberation policies, breaking down barriers between women and men, black and white people, Jews and Arabs, etc. This led to the Women's Movement and involvement with the Jewish Socialist Group and other peace movements.

During my various training courses in psychotherapy, both person-centred counselling and Adlerian psychology, I gained such valuable insights and met wonderful people. The privilege to listen to so many stories and being part of so many groups gave my life a new dimension. I cannot think of more fascinating work.

In spite of living in different countries, Bent and I kept our closeness throughout those difficult years, as well as the good times – and I have loved both his partners: Dorrit and later Aase.

I have learned that when there is a disintegration and an end, there is also a new beginning, and with all that comes new life and new relationships. Creating a life with my husband Philip, our two children, Jan and Nina, the greatest gift of all, and experiencing them finding loving partners, Jonnie and Irene... and with every grandchild – Rachel, Sam, Ben, Hannah, Sophie and Reuben – came tremendous joy and happiness.

Not to forget all those close friendships formed and such wonderful time spent together.

All in all, meaning in life.

My mother with sister Cecilia, Landskrona, 1921; and with bicycle, Landskrona, 1928

My parents in love, Landskrona, 1937; and Copenhagen, 1938

My mother (front left with long plaits) and her schoolfriends, Landskrona, 1929

My father (back row, second from right) in his school photograph with headteacher Mr Pihler, Copenhagen, 1927

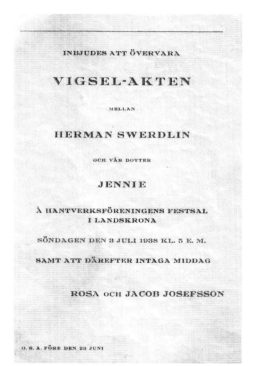

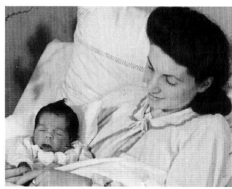

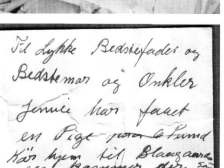

Top right and opposite: My parents' wedding,
3 July 1938 and (top left) the invitation
Above left: Anita just born, 22 September
1940, and (left) a note from my father:
'Congratulations Farfar and Farmor and
uncles. Jennie has had a girl six pounds. Go
home to Blågårds Road. I will go there later'
Above right: My mother and Bent: a special
relationship, Malmø, 1945

My mother and morfar, Landskrona, 1949; my parents, Søvang

Myself, my mother, Bent and my father, 1947

The boss, Finn Christensen, and my father, 1978; (inset) in the Politiken newspaper: 'The foreman of the workshop at Birger Christensen, H Sverdlin, is celebrating 50 years with the firm. Reception at Birger Christensen, Østergade 38, Friday, between 10 and 12'

My father's three beloved grandchildren: Jan, Nina and Rami

4

A LIGHT IN THE DARKNESS

Thousands of Jews escaped on fishing boats from Denmark to Sweden in 1943

4 A Light in the Darkness

My brother Bent and I should not be here today. In October 1943, when the Nazis had planned to capture all the Jews of Denmark and send them to concentration camps, the Danish people carried out the most amazing rescue operation and managed to save nearly 7,000 of their Jewish citizens.

I was three years old, and my parents (my mother being six months pregnant) and my father's sister Poula were betrayed, and we were first sent to Vestre Fængsel, the main prison in Copenhagen, and later to Horserød prison camp in North Sjælland.

Miraculously we were saved at the very last minute. On the same day as all the other Jewish people in Horserød were sent to the concentration camp, Theresienstadt, we were set free because my mother was a Swedish citizen.

Eventually we went to Malmø in neutral Sweden, where Bent was born three months later. Bent and I would never have survived Theresienstadt – and subsequently none of our children and grandchildren would have been born.

Seventy years have passed since the Second World War. Thirty million people died in this War, mostly soldiers in battle, but also anti-fascists, gay people and Gypsies.

Six million Jews in Europe (or two out of every three Jews) were also murdered. They had no graves, many were gassed and then burnt to ashes.

The Holocaust was not like previous persecutions of Jews, which had taken place throughout the ages; the Nazis' goal was to exterminate all the Jewish people, and for the first time in history 'The Final Solution' became the national policy of a so-called 'civilised' European government.

There is one dangerous myth, which now and again resurfaces: that the Jews went to the gas chambers as 'lambs to the slaughterhouse', and that they willingly assisted in their own destruction. Nothing can be further from the truth. This myth was created by the Nazis themselves, who wanted to portray Jewish people as sub-human, so any sign of Jews being brave and fighting back had to be crushed.

The Jews were told to keep a low profile, so they would not draw attention to themselves. They had many problems in getting weapons and armoury from the underground movements, and more often than not, they were rejected when they tried to join resistance fighters and partisan groups. In the ghettos the Jews were starved, suffered epidemics, collective punishment and physical degradation. The greatest number of Jews had nowhere to go; not many countries would let them in, and when they succeeded in escaping, they were often caught by the general surrounding population and handed over to the Nazis.

The crimes of the German Nazis were so unbelievable, so monstrous and inconceivable, that people in general did not take them seriously. The Nazis managed to disguise the deportations as people being sent to workplaces somewhere in the East; and they even planted grass and flowers to camouflage the death camps, so when the refugees arrived, they could quickly and without much resistance get them into the gas chambers to be exterminated.

Even the Allies listened with disbelief to these 'stories' of 'industrial killing' and did nothing militarily to halt the murder.

As Eli Wiesel said: 'The question is not why the Jews did not fight back, but how so many of them did! Tormented, beaten, starved, where did they find the strength, spiritual and physical – to resist?'[1]

And what kind of resistance was possible when a gun was pointed at you while you were carrying your younger children, with the older ones at your side? Escaping from the ghettos was punished by death, but that did not stop the Jews from trying to get away; they even found ways of smuggling food into the ghetto. In the slave factories they sewed the uniforms of the German soldiers back to front, the sleeves or legs inside out or reversed. Before the liquidation of the ghettos, they organised cultural groups and activities for children, so they would suffer as little anxiety as possible. This was carried out to the very end, when the Jews were herded out to the countryside with their children, forced to take off their clothes and dig their own graves. They were shot trying to shelter their children.

'Who would have thought it possible for a Jewish underground organization to exist, let alone function in the very heart of Nazi Germany – Berlin? Yet the Baum-Gruppe, an illegal group composed of young Jewish men and women of varied political persuasions, conducted anti-Nazi activities at the height of the War and under the very noses of the Gestapo.'[2]

Jewish women were among the most courageous fighters. They disguised themselves as non-Jews, dyed their hair and helped to smuggle weapons to the partisan fighters. Names like Rosa Robota and Mala Zimetbaum will never be forgotten. They secretly brought in the dynamite which was used for blowing up one of the crematoriums in Auschwitz and consequently saved the lives of many hundreds of Jewish women.

Zofia Yamaika, only 14 when the War began, printed anti-fascist posters and leaflets, organised illegal study groups in the Warsaw Ghetto and became a leader of an underground resistance movement. She was imprisoned several times, escaped and joined the partisans. She was involved in combat fighting and fell in battle.

Niuta Teitelboim, a woman courier of the Warsaw Ghetto, undertook the most dangerous missions: 'In the ghetto she organised a women's detachment which later produced heroic figures in the Warsaw Ghetto Uprising.'[3]

The courage of these brave fighters will live in our memory forever. There were thousands of them, known and unknown, the evidence found in hidden diaries, scraps of paper tucked away somewhere, and from the survivors themselves all over Europe.

'We waged in many languages the same hard, relentless struggle, a struggle which claimed many victims, and which has not yet ended. The complete eradication of Nazism is our watchword. The building of a new world of peace and freedom is our aim. This we owe to our murdered comrades and their families.' – Oath of the prisoners of Buchenwald, April 1945.[4]

It is in this light that the story of the rescue of the Danish Jews will be told here. It is the story of the human spirit, it is a story about courage and dignity, and what human beings are capable of in adversity. It is indeed a light in the darkness of the Second World War.

The Rescue of Danish Jews

The War in Denmark

The War in Denmark began on 9 April 1940. Very early in the morning, German planes flew in over Denmark and German soldiers invaded from the border in the south of Jylland. The War with Germany was raging all over Europe, but in spite of that, Denmark was not prepared and had hoped to repeat the neutral position it had held during the First World War.

After a few hours' fighting with less than thirty killed or wounded, Denmark capitulated, realising it was a hopeless fight. Denmark was a small country with four and a half million people and its Army stood no chance against the Nazi superpower. Then began the German occupation of Denmark in which the Germans would be in charge of Foreign Affairs, while the Danish Government would be running the Interior Ministry.

There were approximately 7,000 Jewish people in Denmark and they had heard with anxiety what had happened in other European countries invaded by the Germans. Now they found them on their own doorstep. Some panicked and began to think of escape routes; others withdrew their money from the bank and with trepidation waited for further developments. However, right from the start the Jewish population were reassured by the Government that they were Danish citizens, and therefore would be protected.

Jewish people had lived relatively peacefully in Denmark for the last 200 years, and since 1814 they had been given equal legal rights. They were lawful, hard-working citizens, both middle and working class, and many were immigrants from Eastern Europe, mainly Russia and Poland, thirty to forty years earlier. The Danish people in general were not aware of something called a 'Jewish problem' in their country.

There was a small Nazi party in Denmark which got 31,000 votes at the General Election in 1939, and two Nazis became members of the Parliament. After the occupation they became more aggressive and tried to create conflicts by stating that the question about the Jewish people must now be solved.

The Church Minister told the Danish Chief Rabbi, Dr. Friediger, that as long as the Danish Government had a say in this country, the Jews had no grounds for concern.

The year 1940 passed without terror against the Jews, but in November 1941, when the Danish Minister, Eric Scavenius, was called to a meeting in Berlin, one of Hitler's most trusted men, Herman Goring, said that Denmark could not avoid the Jewish problem. Eric Scavenius answered that there was no Jewish problem, because the Danes do not feel inferior! This statement was repeated often by many well-known Danish people.

Denmark was called the Bread-basket of Europe, and Germany needed the Danish dairy and meat products to feed their troops. Germany also wanted to show a model occupation in Denmark, and all these factors contributed to a relatively 'soft policy' toward the population. In 1942 when the 'Final Solution' was decided in Wannsee in Germany, the position of the Danish Jews was simply ignored.

King Christian X was the Danish people's symbol for freedom. He used to ride out daily on his horse from Amalienborg Castle through the streets of Copenhagen without bodyguards, greeting people on the way – and, in defiance, refusing to acknowledge the salutes of the German soldiers. In 1941 when an old synagogue in Ålborg was bombed by the Nazis, he wrote to the Jewish community saying how sorry he was. There are many legends about King Christian X, the best being that if the Jews of Denmark had to wear the yellow star, he would be the first to do so. Just the fact that such a story could be told about him is wonderful.

The decision to collaborate with the Germans did not rest very well with some Danes, and many wondered if they had put up enough of a fight by capitulating after such a short time. Even the Allies were in doubt about Denmark's position. It was not long, though, before the Danes clearly showed their contempt for the Germans – and which side they were on – by increasing acts of sabotage against the military and industrial installations. The Resistance Movement grew in strength, and the fighters were in contact with England, who parachuted weapons in for them. They bombed factories and shops which collaborated with the Germans.

The Jews found themselves in a strange situation. They were happy that people were resisting the Germans, but simultaneously feared the possibility of a break-up between the Germans and the Danish Government, the latter being their shield against persecution. The Jews were told to keep a low profile and not to give the Germans any excuse to persecute them. They lived under the same conditions as other Danes, with ration cards, blackouts, sirens and lack of food, but as yet no-one had been arrested.

Sadly the situation in Norway was very different. On 26 October 1942, Jewish men and boys over 15 years of age were arrested, and one month later women and children were also captured. They tried to warn as many people as possible, but the Germans used sirens all through the night, so no-one was able to venture outside. The next morning 582 Jewish people were taken on board S/S Donau in the harbour of Oslo and sent to Auschwitz Concentration Camp. The ship went south along the Swedish coast, even refuelling in Sweden. Out of a total of 762 deported Norwegian Jews, only 23 returned. A further 700 managed to flee to Sweden across snowy mountains.

Some young Jewish people in Denmark did not like the advice of keeping a low profile and remaining passive. They were mostly young Jewish refugees, who had fled to Denmark before the War, when the persecution of Jews began in Germany. There every Jewish woman was forced to take on the name Sarah and all men Israel, and a big red J was stamped on their papers. Approximately 330,000 Jewish people fled from Germany; the USA, Argentina and England received the greatest number of refugees.

There are numerous heartbreaking stories of Jewish people trying to enter neighbouring countries from Germany, but time after time they were turned away, had nowhere to go, and in their despair were forced to go back to Germany.

Sadly Denmark did not do much to help the German Jews, for one reason and another they did not consider their plight serious enough. 4,500 refugees passed through Denmark in the 1930s, but only 1,500 were allowed to stay.

Britain on the other hand received many children on the Kindertransport. They were fostered out with different families, or if they were old enough they became domestic servants. Rarely did they see their parents again.

The Danish Government gave permission for 350 young people to stay in Denmark where they would learn agriculture and then travel to Palestine. Some of them were eager to fight the Germans; they had already lost their family and did not want to be caught by the Germans like 'sheep to the slaughter'. So they planned an escape route south through Europe to Turkey and Palestine by strapping themselves underneath a train. Nearly everyone was arrested and sent to Auschwitz. Only one survived.

Hitler was increasingly angry that the Jews of Denmark had avoided deportation, so in 1943 he sent a new General to Denmark by the name of Werner Best. He was responsible for killing thousands of Jews in Poland and planning and carrying out many deportations of Jews to concentration camps. His nickname was the 'Butcher of Paris', and he personally sent hundreds of Jewish children from Drancey to their deaths.

Best was briefed by his predecessor Von Renthe Fink, and understood that it was in Germany's interest to continue with the 'soft' policy in Denmark to avoid conflicts – and most importantly to safeguard the supply of Danish food to Germany.

During the summer of 1943, the Allies won victories on all fronts, more and more Danes dared openly to carry out sabotage, strikes and demonstrations – and a general strike followed. Best got strict orders from Berlin to put down the resistance, and on 28 August 1943, he ordered the Government to declare Denmark in a state of emergency. The Danish Government felt they could no longer meet the demands of the German occupiers, and they resigned. The Germans arrested the Danish police, soldiers and officers, and the King and his family were prisoners in the castle. It was forbidden to hold meetings, no-one was allowed to go out after dark, the press was censored, and there was a death penalty for sabotage.

On 29 August 1943, the Chief Rabbi Friediger and other leaders of the Jewish community were arrested, and on 17 September, German soldiers broke into the Jewish Community Centre and confiscated the list of all the Jewish people in Denmark. In hindsight this was a very serious warning indeed, but still no precautions were taken.

Best continued to deny that any action was planned against the Jews. He played a very sly, double role, and secretly, to please Hitler, he sent a telegram to Berlin stating his intention of arresting all the Jews of Denmark, women and children included, and demanding big ships from Germany to transport them from the harbour of Copenhagen. All along he was considering his own position in Denmark as the good guy, in case Germany lost the War. He knew very well how strongly the Danish authorities and the population in general were against any persecution of the Jews.

Best confided in George Duckwitz, a German, who had lived in Denmark for several years, was part of the German envoy and worked in shipping. Duckwitz was shocked and horrified, and deeply ashamed of this secret plan against the Danish Jews. His first response was to leave his post, but being a man of action and a true human being, he decided to go to Berlin to try and stop the telegram reaching Hitler. He was too late. He immediately went to Stockholm in Sweden and asked the Government there if they would receive Danish Jewish refugees.

Sweden's position during the War was very ambivalent. It was neutral, but many Swedes sympathised with the Germans (and the idea of a superior, blonde Aryan race), and it allowed Germany to use its railways for carrying supplies and troops to Norway. Not only that, at the beginning of the War, Sweden refused to be a base for the Danish Resistance, and some Swedes earned a great deal of money, especially in the steel industry, by dealing with the Germans.

However, in 1943, as the wind turned and a possibility of Germany losing the War emerged, Sweden developed a more anti-German policy, and from September 1943 they refused to allow the Germans to use their railways. The Swedish Government therefore promised that they would receive the Danish Jews, if the possibility of a flight across Øresund arose.

The secret plan of the Germans was a raid on all Jewish homes on the night of 1 October 1943, which was the festival of the Jewish New Year, Rosh Hashana, when they could be sure that the Jewish people would be at home.

Duckwitz, the unforgettable hero of these days, wasted no time. He immediately gave the message to a politician, the Social Democrat, Hans Hedtoft, who personally contacted the leader of the Jewish community, CB Henriques. His first reaction was disbelief, but it did not take long before the message was given to Rabbi Marcus Melchior. From the pulpit in the synagogue the congregation were warned in advance that they must go home and make preparations to hide – and they must not be at home on the night of 1 October. The message got round like wildfire: every Jewish person tried to contact as many people as possible. Sometimes the warning came from a non-Jew, a head teacher, doctor or friend.

People had to make their own arrangements. Some went into hiding with their neighbours, others contacted their 'safe' friends or relations, some hid with the teacher from their children's school – or the baker round the corner. It had to happen quickly and there was little time to make decisions.

Some Jewish families in their panic just ran out of their houses and tried to hide in the forests near the coast. Some felt there was no way out and took poison. Some were shot in front of their children. The young people were mostly full of courage and determination, but the elderly, some sick and weak, were more stubborn and wanted to remain at home. Jewish people who had earlier arrived as refugees did not have the strength to flee again – and others just hoped that they would not be found.

Werner Best had ordered the Gestapo from Germany to be the leaders of the raid, and they were the most brutal. Thirty-seven people lost their lives during the first night. As an example of the Nazis' extreme brutal and cowardly behaviour, they went first for the old people, who were not able to run away or defend themselves.

Behind the synagogue in Krystalgade was the Jewish Old Age Home, and they dragged the old people out – some blind and senile, others carried out half-naked in sheets and thrown on the cattle trucks. Their families, if they had any, were all in hiding or fleeing the country; no provision was made for the old people's rescue. Through the night in the streets of Copenhagen you could hear heartbroken cries and screams.

But during the first night of the raid, the Germans had only been able to catch 264 out of 7,000 Jews. The action against the Jews had not succeeded, and they had not even been able to fill one of the two big cargo ships which were ready to transport the Jews to Germany. The SS in Berlin was furious and in shock, and Hitler had a tantrum. The reality was that more than 90% of Jewish people were still in hiding.

During the next 24 hours something amazing happened. Without any order from the Danish officials, the general population formed spontaneous groups, each of which worked alone. They looked up Jewish people, hid them in private homes, sometimes in several places; they arranged cars to take them to the coast and found fishermen who would sail them across to Sweden in the night. The medical and hospital services took Jewish people in as patients, gave them false names, put bandages round them, so no-one would be able to notice their dark complexions, put them in beds, on operating tables and in the morgues. Ambulances drove them around and taxi services also transported people from place to place. The University closed for a week, so the students would be able to help. It was one thing hiding the Jews, another to transport them to the coast and then find a fisherman who would take them across to Sweden in the night.

One such helping group was called 'Holger Danske' after the famous Viking, whose statue is in Kronborg Castle. The legend tells us that when Denmark is in trouble, Holger Danske will come to life and help Denmark. The group Holger Danske was led by the 20-year-old Ebba Lund, who in 1943 managed to get more than 500 Jewish people to safety in Sweden. Wearing a red beret, she was also given the name Red Ridinghood.[5]

Officially she was an expert chef, trading in Danish goods. The communications and arrangements, to move refugees around and finally find a boat to take them, were made to sound like trading in sacks of potatoes for restaurants – quantities and where to deliver them.

In the daily newspaper was an illegal column, 'Exchange Central', which gave messages in code to the helpers as to where on the coast there would be boats for the refugees. No-one questioned the fact that the Jews had to pay for seats on the boat, which cost between 1,000 kr and 5,000 kr; it was a fortune in those days, and the Jews had to sell their belongings very quickly, but no-one complained. They were not used to strangers taking a risk for their sake. The skipper or fisherman risked his livelihood or arrest, so that was only fair.

No-one was left behind, and an anonymous Dane paid for 180 seats. The medical profession collected a big sum of money, as did various other groups, and a former minister in the Government managed to fetch money that was at the disposal of the Danish authorities.

The Germans announced that as a gesture of goodwill for arresting the Jews – who in any case were corrupt, responsible for all the sabotage and anti-German feeling etc – they would now release all the Danish soldiers who had been arrested. An outcry erupted from the Danish people over the proposal; they protested, felt scorn and contempt and would not accept such a trading of human beings. Sympathy for the Jews was deep and genuine and there was protest from the King, the political parties and the unions.

However, the great majority who went out of their way to help were not the famous, but ordinary Danes. They were ready to fight the Gestapo, the world's most hideous and best organised police power, and in doing so they were given a role in this bloody world drama over 2,000 years which is the history of anti-semitism.

On 3 October 1943, in all the churches all over Denmark, the priests read the same script from the pulpit:

'We understand religious freedom as the right to serve God, and that race and religion can never be a cause to deprive a person's rights, freedom and home. We will fight so that our Jewish brothers and sisters preserve the same freedom which we consider more precious than life itself.'[6]

Many priests issued false christening certificates for people staying behind, and hundreds of Jews hid in vicarages, churches and with priests and bishops. Other hiding places were children's homes, colleges and high schools.

Doctors often gave sedatives to young children before the crossing – and while it was all happening, some German soldiers turned their backs and pretended they did not see.

Duckwitz never stopped trying to help. He had ordered the German coast patrol boats to go into repair, and although the Danish coast police were forced to work with the Germans, they deliberately turned a blind eye – and even helped where they could.

In the beginning, personal contact played an important role, but gradually, as the rescue operation got more organised, it did not matter. The refugees were moved many times, as nobody dared to put them up for more than a few days. Danish informers, although not many in number, were still around trying to track down refugees. Just one could do enormous damage, as it turned out.

The stretch from Vedbæk to Snekkersten was especially suitable for crossing, but it was dangerous to use the same routes several times. From the harbours of Hornbæk and Gilleleje, bigger boats were leaving and hundreds of refugees fled to those areas. It was becoming quite a problem, and in Gilleleje at one stage, 90 Jewish people hid in the local church. They were betrayed by a German girl, and they were all sent to Theresienstadt Concentration Camp.

It was not always easy to find a boat, and some Jews had to travel south to Lolland and Falster. This turned out to be a more dangerous crossing, further away from Sweden and nearer the German coast. Not everyone succeeded in reaching the Swedish coastline, and some boats drifted the wrong way in the dark and were picked up by German patrol boats. Others were only able to get hold of a rowing boat and, never having held an oar before, found rowing very difficult – not to mention in fog and high winds. There are heartbreaking stories of Jewish people throwing young children with name tags into the sea to be picked up by Swedish sailors just before they were overrun by a German patrol boat. Every journey was a drama, and over 60 people lost their lives during the crossing.

To bring young children to Sweden could be a problem. They had to be extremely quiet but were often unpredictable. Some parents were advised or genuinely believed that it would be safer to leave them in Denmark, especially if they were blonde and fair and did not look too Jewish. They were put into orphanages or looked after by non-Jewish friends and relatives. The decision had to be taken quickly and was often regretted, causing lifelong traumas for some, both parents and children.

It was all done in good faith and with the best intentions and the non-Jewish families sincerely reached out and tried to help the best they could.

Nevertheless, for various reasons (perhaps the risk of keeping them in Denmark turned out to be too serious or the children were suffering severe loss and separation anxiety), some of the children were later brought over to Sweden during the night in small fishing boats, often heavily sedated, to be united with their parents.

More children stayed behind than was previously thought; it caused such guilt and shame for the parents that they could not talk about it. Owing to this silence and secrecy, the children made up their own personal, often hurtful reasons for being left behind and mistrusted that adults could take care of them – or indeed wanted them. That it was the 'best' solution to leave them behind was the adults' reasoning, not the children's, and they had difficulty in accepting the adults' choice.[7]

However, during those dark and fateful October nights in 1943, the psychological consequences were far from people's minds as the Danes put enormous efforts into getting their Jewish citizens across to Sweden, whether they were children or adults. One eyewitness remembers seeing wooden boxes that looked like cargo and goods, but actually contained sedated Jewish babies being transported onto a fishing boat.

Funeral processions suddenly became very popular, as a way of carrying Jewish families, with the curtains drawn in the cars, to safe hiding places or to a destination on the coast, where a boat was ready to take them to Sweden. Creativity seems to have been in great supply during those days.

My family had kept a low profile like other Jewish people; some of them, like my mother's brother Henning, his wife Bertha and young son Bertil, had already decided to move to Sweden in 1942.

According to my cousin Cecil, who was 15 years old, his father, my mother's eldest brother Herman, got involved in the Resistance Movement when he was a patient at Bispebjerg Hospital. This was very unusual and not encouraged. If you were caught, it would give the Germans an excuse to persecute the Jews. Nevertheless my uncle was arrested three times and spent some time in prison where he contracted tuberculosis, and he died in May 1942. My cousin Cecil continued to work with the Resistance, giving out leaflets until he had to flee to Sweden.

The news of the raid first reached my parents through my grandfather. He rushed to my father's workplace, told him the news and urged him to go into hiding straight away. Some of my father's work colleagues overheard the conversation and were horrified. They offered to help in any way they could, promising to go to our flat in Kretavej 49 on Amager to pack up our belongings and take care of them.

It was obvious that the whole family could not go together and there was no way we could communicate with each other. My paternal grandparents and my two uncles, Max and Oscar, were hiding with Knud's uncle. My grandmother was in a desperate state: she just could not believe that she had to flee like this; she had bad memories from Russia, and now she had to leave her home again. She had always felt so safe in Denmark before the Germans invaded.

Vera and Ernest were hiding with their non-Jewish friends, Lis and Helge Ferrold. Vera recalls being woken up early one morning by Lis and Helge to listen to the news: there had been a raid on all the Jewish homes; the Germans had only been able to capture a few hundred Jews, but they issued strong warnings to the Danes assisting and hiding the Jews. Vera was terribly worried about her parents and siblings, so Lis and Helge rode out on their bikes to Knud's uncle and were later able to reassure Vera that nothing had happened to them. Vera and Ernest spent eight days with the Ferrolds, who both went out to work every day. During the day they felt so powerless and apathetic, listening out for the Gestapo on the stairs.

Helge was trying to organise a boat which would take the whole family to Sweden. After eight days, Vera and Ernest were told to be ready the following night. A taxi picked them up and took them to Amager beach, where they were united with her parents and brothers, who wore big hats to cover their dark curly hair. Vera was wearing a red wig, and she would later wonder how naive she had been – how could she disguise who she was? Forty refugees went on board, among them Ernest's parents and family – all sitting silently at the bottom of the boat. They had all paid the skipper a huge amount of money for each person. When they reached the Swedish fairway, Ernest asked the skipper to send a message to Ferrold stating that everyone was safe. But the skipper told Ferrold that Ernest had not paid his fare (which was not true), so Ferrold had to pay 1,000 kr extra.

The Ferrolds were never forgotten by the Isacksens. After the War they were invited to all the family celebrations, paid homage to and applauded at every possible occasion.

My parents, my aunt Poula and I were hiding with a Swedish friend of my mother's. She had a house near my parents' flat, and we saw a great deal of her and her family before the War. They had a big cellar where we spent several days before a rescue group helped us to get to the coast. It was the middle of the night when we got the message that a fishing boat on Amager near Kastrup was ready to take us. It was only a small boat, and we were approximately ten people. We had dressed very warmly with several layers of clothes on top of each other. How were we to know if we would ever see our home again?

The tension was high, and we were extremely nervous. My father carried me; being only three years old, I did not understand the severity of what we were doing. I was told not to make a sound. We went in a line onto the bridge and were told to sit down quietly at the lower deck. We had brought money with us and each had to pay the fisherman 2,000 kr.

When we had all settled down, somebody suddenly shouted: 'The Germans are coming, they have seen us!' In a panic we all ran out of the boat onto the shore and into the nearest shed on the beach. I was screaming and my mother put a handkerchief in my mouth. It was to no avail. The Germans had seen us and surrounded the shed. It was a terrible moment – they had dogs and guns.

Poula was the last person to leave the shed; she tried to stay behind and talk to one of the Germans. She asked him if he would let her go free, saying she would give him all the money she had. She also told him that she had just got married and that she would give him nice things from her flat. He seemed interested but then another German entered and shouted, 'All out!'

Big cattle trucks were ready to take us away; my parents and I stood close together, my father carrying me, trying to calm me down. Several Danish policemen were there, powerless to help. Some of them were crying. My aunt Poula asked one of the Nazi women if my mother could go free – she pointed at my mother and said: 'Can't you see she is expecting a child?' The woman just did a sign with her hand and said: 'Get into that truck.'

At that moment Poula's husband Knud came cycling with a friend onto the beach. He was horrified to see his wife and us being taken away like this, and in his desperation he wanted to run towards us. His friend had a real fight to restrain him – he would have been shot. This scene became a nightmare for my aunt, who relived the episode again and again. It woke her up in the night, and she had several breakdowns, until late in her life when she was helped by a psychologist.

We were taken to the main prison in Copenhagen, Vestre Fængsel. Women and children were herded into one room, and we did not know what had happened to the men. I screamed and ran up to the gate, banged my fists and shouted: 'I want to go home, let me out, I am cold.' My mother was outwardly very calm and she tried to reassure me. She kept this composure all the time for my sake, so I would not be frightened.

The men were all being interrogated individually. When it was my father's turn and they asked him his name, he answered Herman Sverdlin. They shouted: 'Your name is not Herman, it is Moses.' When they asked him again and he said Herman, they screamed at him: 'No, you are Moses.' When they asked him a third time, he answered Moses. He had seen how they had beaten up another man who didn't do what he was told. Obviously they did not want my father's name to be Herman. Herman Goring was one of the top Nazis in Germany.

They wanted to humiliate the men as much as possible. They did the same with the women. They made us run around like chickens and make sounds – and then they laughed at us. We were also forced to stand up against the wall with our hands up. My mother told me it was a game, so I would not be worried. The food was mostly some kind of muddy soup, and we had to sleep on the bare floor.

One night Poula rang a bell and when the woman guard came in, Poula said: 'Look, my sister-in-law is going to give birth, she doesn't feel well, she must go to the hospital.' The guard just laughed loudly, right into Poula's face.

Some of the women were very religious and they prayed. It was coming up to Yom Kippur, the holiest of Jewish festivals. Poula lost her temper and screamed at them: 'How can you pray, can't you see there is no God?'

After a few days in Vestre Fængsel we were taken to a camp in North Sjælland called Horserød. It was a prison camp for Resistance fighters, Communists and Jewish people, all waiting to be transported to the concentration camp, Theresienstadt, in Czechoslovakia. My parents had not seen each other for days, and had feared the worst; the reunion was very emotional and they were grateful for small mercies.

In Horserød, the young prisoners had to help build new barracks for the growing number of prisoners. Poula was helped to lift a plank by a young German soldier but my father was furious with her – allowing a Nazi to help her!

Werner Best kept playing his double role. His personal intention was to make Denmark free of Jews, but to pacify the growing protest from the Danish public servants and government officials (who felt there were no legal rights, when Danish citizens could be hunted in this manner), he issued a guarantee that people who were only half Jewish or were married to a non-Jew could go free.

And so Poula was free to leave the camp, together with ten other Jews in a similar situation.

My mother's Swedish friend seemed to have had some important German connections. She contacted Knud, and together they went to the German Headquarters, Dagmarhus. Knud was told that Poula should refrain from trying to flee the country again; if she was captured once more she would be shot. Poula was taken to the central square in Copenhagen, Rådhuspladsen, and from there she went to Knud's parents.

She was 'free', but she could not go out anywhere. She was so dark and foreign looking, she did not dare to show herself outside. The strain was too much, the terrible experience she had been through – and now this. She had a nervous breakdown and the doctor advised her to flee to Sweden. This time she succeeded, and Knud remained in Copenhagen working as a tram conductor.

My parents and I remained in the prison camp. It was not like a concentration camp in Germany or elsewhere in Europe – we were not tortured and we were given some food – but everyone knew it was only a matter of time before we would be deported. The strain was unbearable, and the mood of the people very low.

The news that Poula, my parents and I had been captured was given to my paternal grandmother (farmor) after a frightening trip across the sea. She had just put her first foot on Swedish soil when a young man came running towards her and gave her the message. In her anguish she wanted to throw herself into the sea, and a Swedish priest sat with her all night to comfort her. My grandfather (farfar) suffered a psychotic episode. He just could not take in this terrible news and behaved like a doorman in the refugee centre in Sweden, standing at the door letting people in and out. It was only for a short time.

When my mother's parents received the news, my grandmother ran to the park and banged her head repeatedly against a tree. My grandfather went to a Swedish lawyer to enquire what could be done. My mother had been a Swedish citizen before she married my father, and on account of Sweden's neutral position in the War, they applied for her to be reinstated as a Swedish citizen.

That saved our lives. The decision was actually made by the Swedish Government, but what we shall never know is how much money my grandfather had to pay for this deal. There are all kinds of rumours from various family members, but whatever the demand, it would have been paid.

So on the very same day as the other Jewish people, sadly, were transported to Theresienstadt, we were free to leave the camp. Somehow we managed to get back to Copenhagen where we stayed with our non-Jewish friends. My mother and I were now legitimate Swedish citizens, and very quickly we managed to travel to Sweden legally. We went to Landskrona, and the reunion with all the family was indescribable – screams and tears of joy.

My father had to stay in Copenhagen to apply for Swedish citizenship. It was a very dangerous time: the Danish Government had dispersed, the country was in a state of emergency, the Germans were in full control and there were no Jewish people around. My father went around Copenhagen on his bike with a big hat covering his dark hair, and claimed he had no fear now, knowing my mother and I were safe in Sweden.

He had to go to the German Headquarters itself, Dagmarhus, to get his Swedish documents, and there was always the chance that the Germans would arrest him again. He brought with him a Danish friend in uniform. He knew that the Germans respected uniforms, even if it was only a Home Guard. It was not an easy task. My father had to go from office to office, explaining the situation that he was married to a Swedish citizen, and in the end he got his papers.

He could now travel legally to Sweden, and Knud went with him to the ferry, which would take him across to Malmø. Fear or no fear, sweat was dripping from my father's forehead. Knud would never forget this terrifying moment. They both knew that the Germans could easily, if it suited them, tear up the papers. My father got on the ferry, and two hours later he was safely in Sweden.

My parents and I had only been a fraction away from being deported to Theresienstadt like the rest of the 464 Danish Jews. Their journey to Theresienstadt in Czechoslovakia had been a nightmare. They had spent 24 hours at the bottom of a big ship without food. Among them were some of the very old and infirm people who were dragged out of the Old Age Home during the first night of the raid. They were totally in shock and disorientated and whimpered in their misery. The Danish Jews spent the next three days on a cattle train, so tightly packed they were hardly able to sit down. People were sick and fainted, and they wondered what crime they had committed to deserve this.

Before the War, Theresienstadt had been an Army barrack town for 7,000 Czech citizens, but as the War progressed they were ordered to leave, and it became a concentration camp for 50,000 Jewish people, who all had to wear the yellow star.

Hunger and sickness were the worst. People had to queue up for hours for something which resembled soup. It was made out of rotten potato peel and other scraps. You were given half a loaf of bread a week, a little bit of sugar and margarine, but you never experienced the feeling of fullness.

'The hunger overshadowed everything, it was growing constantly in the stomach day and night. Everyone knows the feeling of being hungry. But to starve day after day, week after week, month after month... the long ongoing hunger...'[8]

The old people died quickly, some gave up and starved themselves to death. Nearly everyone had diarrhoea; fleas and bedbugs were everywhere, biting, smelly and dangerous, causing disease and infection.

'33,500 Jewish people died during a period of three to four years – and that was exactly the intention of the Nazis.'[9]

In the midst of all this deplorable degradation, the children were the Jewish people's highest priority. It was forbidden to teach them, but occupying them was allowed, so various games were played and in between those the children did maths, history and languages.

The Nazis were obsessed with numbers and counting the Jews, and frequently, at four o'clock in the morning, they had to assemble outside the barracks in the freezing cold. This could go on for hours; everyone had to attend and many collapsed. It was impossible to escape.

However, the Danish Jews in Theresienstadt were not forgotten. The Danish King Christian X wrote to them personally that they were in his thoughts and prayers, and the Danish Red Cross sent them food parcels. Without these extra supplies of food, the Danish Jews would not have survived. It was such a boost for them, it strengthened their morale and gave them tremendous encouragement, to know that they were not forgotten and that others were thinking of them.

Jewish people were sent to Theresienstadt from all over Europe, from Germany, Holland, France and Denmark, and although there were no gas chambers, from Theresienstadt the Jews were sent to other death camps to be exterminated. That did not happen to the Danish Jews, but they never knew they would not be deported, and like all the other European Jews they lived in constant fear that their name or any of their children's or families' or loved ones' names would be on that dreaded list for deportation.

People were fighting to have their names taken off the list – you were fighting for your lives, to be moved on to the 'protected' list – but even then you were only safe temporarily, as tomorrow there would be a new list. A special group was appointed to decide whose name was going to be put on that list, and the Nazis made the Jews do their dirty work for them, by forcing some Jewish elders to choose the names. For example, the order might be for a certain number of orphaned children, blind people or German and Dutch citizens. They were told they would build a new town for them, and the families would be united again. People wanted to believe to the very last. In the end the Jewish elders ended up in the gas chambers like everybody else.

The fact that the Danish Jews were not to be deported only became clear to them at the end of the War, but that decision had already been taken on 2 November 1943 by the Danish Red Cross and representatives from the Danish authorities and signed by Werner Best himself, who without doubt was planning his escape route. (After the War he avoided the death penalty and only served a mild prison sentence.)

The Danish authorities asked to make a visit to Theresienstadt in order to check on the Danish Jews. It took place in June 1944, and among the delegates were ministers from the Health Department, the Foreign Office and Danish Red Cross.

Just before the visit, the Nazis made the camp look more presentable: 7,500 Jews, the most sick and emaciated, were sent to the gas chambers in Auschwitz. Shops were quickly set up full of food, the post office gave out parcels, and people were ordered to sit at tables and drink coffee.

'On the day, the old and sick were not allowed on the street. They built a children's pavilion in beautiful colours, and the children were instructed to shout: "Oh Uncle Rahm [Rahm was the SS Camp Chief], are we going to eat sardines again now?"'[10]

The most beautiful of the Jewish girls performed a play, and a football match took place. The prisoners were strictly watched and warned not to talk to the visitors or tell them the truth. You wonder how the Danish delegates could have been fooled to that extent! However, one of the delegates gave a personal greeting from the Danish King to Chief Rabbi Friediger that he was sincerely thinking of them. That greeting spread like wildfire to all the Danish Jews with the words: 'Uncle Christian is very well,' and it gave them hope and courage.

The next day it was all gone, and the people who had taken part were all deported; even the young children were sent to Auschwitz. In 1944, 20,000 went to the gas chambers.

A month before the War ended, on 15 April 1945, the Danish Jews were brought home in the famous 'white buses', an initiative from the Swedish Count Bernadotte, who organised the Swedish Red Cross to pick them up and drive them through Europe to Denmark. Out of the 464 deported Danish Jews, 410 survived, thanks to the Danish authorities' stubborn and democratic efforts and contribution.

When the Allies and the Russians were gaining ground in the Nazi-occupied countries, the Germans tried to remove all traces of their crime in the concentration camps. They sent the prisoners on the death march, where thousands died. There seemed to be no end to the cruelty of the Nazis.

On 9 May 1945, the Russian Army entered Theresienstadt and liberated the camp.

My family never forgot how lucky we were. That feeling of escaping disaster and death gave life a certain meaning, a certain importance, as if it had been a gift to which we had to contribute. It was certainly not a feeling of guilt, but rather a commitment and responsibility to life and the Jewish people.

At first we lived at a special housing centre for refugees from all over Europe, but eventually we got a flat of our own in Malmø, in Gustaf Rydbergsgatan 14A. We were, after all, Swedish citizens. It took the Swedish authorities only three days before my father got his call-up papers from the Air Force. The irony was that my father had been exempt from service in Denmark, because he was very near-sighted. He applied to live at home on account of my mother's ill health from the War experience, but he was refused, although he was allowed to come home at weekends.

Our Danish family were all moved to different places in Sweden. My grandparents lived in Tyringe; Max went to Stockholm to work for a Swedish newspaper; Oscar went to Göteborg to continue his apprenticeship as an electrician. He lived with a Swedish family and went to a technical college in the evening (he was only 16).

Poula moved to Helsingborg and worked in a children's clothes shop in Drottningsgatan. She served in the shop and also worked as a seamstress. She received special messages from Knud from the Resistance people, who came illegally to Sweden. It could be a coded message, and she put an advertisement in the Danish newspaper, *Politiken*: 'All well Poula.' She also received the message that the informer who had betrayed us was shot by the Danish Resistance.

We nearly always had people staying with us during those two and a half years in Malmø. People slept on the floor or on put-up beds in our little flat, in the lounge, in the kitchen and hall. They were mainly refugees from Poland or other European countries; some of them came from concentration camps or slave labour camps, and somehow they managed to get to neutral Sweden. One such couple was called Adler. They got separated in Lodz Ghetto, and each believed the other had perished in the camps. Meeting each other by chance in Malmø was like a miracle. They married and had a baby, and they stayed with us for a while.

I listened to all these stories, how people cried with joy and happiness, and I also listened to people who had lost everything and every one of their family. There seemed to be people surrounding us constantly, people telling their stories, and in my own way as a three- to five-year-old, I listened and tried to make sense of it.

My brother Bent was born on 29 January 1944. All the family were there: grandparents from both sides, aunts, uncles and friends – the whole of the Jewish community in Malmø seemed to be present at his Brit-Milah (circumcision) – and to celebrate the fantastic rescue of our family.

When my father finished his Air Force service he was offered a partnership in a fur shop in Malmø, but after the War, Birger Christensen wanted him back and my mother was happy to return to Denmark.

There was a mystery surrounding my mother's Swedish friend in whose cellar we had been hiding. We did not see her after the War, and some people believed she received vital information from the Germans. Money was also involved. Was she a spy or was she a double agent?

When the War ended in Denmark on 4 May 1945, the Danish Jews in Malmø walked down to the harbour with burning torches, so they could look over to free Denmark. Whilst Bent was asleep in his pram, my parents and I took part in the celebrations, and as a special treat I was able to stay up late that night. It was a very emotional evening. A band was playing the Danish National Anthem and other well-known Danish songs, and the atmosphere was jubilant and joyful – until a ship arrived with refugees from the concentration camps. Sick and emaciated, barely alive Jewish survivors, some carried out on stretchers, emerged from the ship.

The band stopped playing and people just cried, with such mixed emotions: joy and relief that the War had finally ended, and then utter despair and sorrow in witnessing what price Jewish people had paid in this War.

My parents, Bent and I stayed on in Sweden for more than six months after the War ended. We were now Swedish citizens and had to reapply for Danish citizenship. On the other hand nearly all the Danish Jews – my grandparents, aunts and uncles included – returned to Denmark fairly quickly, and most of them (there were exceptions) found their belongings had been packed away and stored for them and their homes looked after. (It was very different for other European Jews. The few who returned to their home towns found nothing there and it was often as if they had never existed. Many survivors spent the next few years in transit camps with nowhere to go.)

Big ships were hired to bring the Danish Jews home, and large banners were displayed in Copenhagen harbour which read: *Welcome Home!*

Notes

1. *They Fought Back*, edited and translated by Yuri Suhl, Schocken Books, New York, 1975 (p.4).
2. Ibid (p.1).
3. Ibid (p.52).
4. *The Yellow Star*, Gerhard Schoenberner, Butler & Tanner, Frome and London, 1969 (p.212).
5. *Jødisk Orientering* 10/83, Jewish community journal (p.70).
6. *Et Folk Paa Flugt: De Danske Jøder under Anden Verdenskrig (A People Fleeing: The Danish Jews in the Second World War)*, Grethe Segal, Forlag Gyldendal, 1991 (Proclamation p.43).
7. *Politiken* newspaper, 2009.
8. *Theresienstadt*, teaching material published by Danmarks Radio, 1983 (p.11).
9. Ibid (p.11).
10. Ibid (p.14).

Right: The German helper, George Ferdinand Duckwitz (1904–73)

Below: The Swedish citizenship document that saved us

B E V I S
angående upptagande till svensk medborgare.

Danska medborgaren Jenny Sverdlin, född Josefsson, som är född den 13 december 1913 i Landskrona och för närvarande har sitt hemvist i Köpenhamn, har anhållit att bliva upptagen till svensk medborgare.

I ärendet är upplyst, att sökanden i äktenskap med danske medborgaren Herman Hirsch Sverdlin har dottern Anita Eva, född den 22 september 1940.

I anledning av ansökningen hava sökandens man ävensom Kungl. Maj:ts minister i Köpenhamn avgivit yttranden.

K U N G L . M A J : T har genom beslut denna dag upptagit sökanden till svensk medborgare.

Tillika har Kungl. Maj:t bestämt att sökandens upptagande till svensk medborgare skall medföra svenskt medborgarskap jämväl för hennes ovan omförmälda dotter.

Om vad sålunda förekommit länder detta till bevis.

Stockholm i justitiedepartementet den 8 oktober 1943.

(Thorwald Bergquist)

S T Ä M P E L 40 K R O N O R .

(Ragnar Kihlgren)

82

Below is a letter my father wrote to Poula from Horserød prison camp. Poula had just been released because she was married to a non-Jewish man, Knud Larsen. It reads:

Dear Poula,
We are all well, but I write to you to ask you if you could send Anita's warm dress and cardigan, and one doll and some other toy and Anita's winter boots.
Send also Jennie's shoes, slip, vest, darning wool for socks, sewing thread and needles.
And for me send one pair of trousers, one shirt and handkerchief, and some tobacco, if you can and one set of underwear.
Send also some fruit and some chocolate, a packet of soap powder, and one bar of soap for Anita.
Lots of love to all
from Jennie, Anita
and Herman
P.S. You can send it all in the brown suitcase.

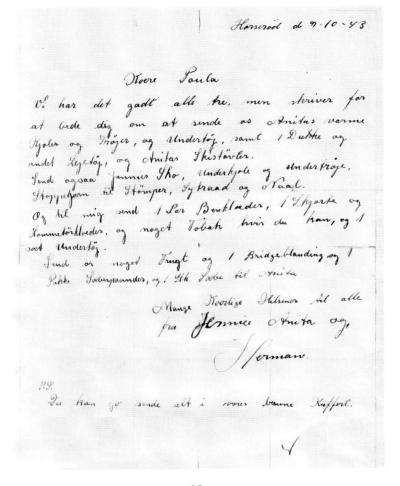

This page, from top:
My parents and I, Copenhagen,
1943 and (below) 1941;
on the beach in Malmø, 1945

Opposite, from top left: Bent on
Max's shoulders; myself and Bent;
my grandparents and parents, Max,
Oscar holding Bent, and me in
front, 1945

EPILOGUE

King Christian X in Copenhagen

Epilogue

I am often asked the question: Why did this level of resistance to the Nazis happen in Denmark and not in other European countries?

But the question we need to ask ourselves is rather: How could the Holocaust have happened at all? How was it conceivable that in one of the most sophisticated and intellectually developed parts of Europe, which had produced sublime music, beautiful art and great philosophers – how was it possible that this industrial mass killing of people could take place?

It was not as if the smoke of the crematoriums could not be seen miles away, so why were they not bombed? Or the railway tracks leading up to the concentration camps?

The unfortunate answer is that the ground was already laid for this to happen: almost two thousand years of anti-Semitism.

The fact that it did not happen in Denmark, and that people stood up to the Nazi monstrosities, was because support for the Jewish people came from the top: the King and the Government and the Danish Christian churches, which were all united; the churches were indeed an exception to what happened in other countries.

The Danish population generally thought it a crime to persecute the Jewish people, whom they considered Danish citizens just like everyone else. They would have done the same for the Scouts or any other group. The geographical circumstances also helped, with neutral Sweden just across the sea.

Neutral Switzerland on the other hand did not accept many refugees, which sadly meant they were turned back and perished in the gas chambers.

A great deal has been written about the many Germans in Denmark who turned a blind eye; they will be remembered always.

The years from 1943 to 1945 shaped my life, and my most passionate ambition from when I was ten years old was to live in Israel. It only lasted three years; in the final instance people are more important than countries.

From a very early age I could not bear to watch injustices, bullying, prejudice or racism. I had to stand up against it, often to my own detriment and risking a great deal. Joining political groups and peace movements became such an important factor and gave my life a special meaning.

For years I dreamed about hiding, and within the family we often talked about where we could hide and with whom. There always seemed to be some danger lurking behind the corner and we could imagine a brick coming through the window. I managed to keep these fears at bay; however, what turned out to be more difficult was my anxiety around tests and exams. My parents did not put pressure on me in that direction, so why did I worry so much? I have finally let go of my promise never to fail so I could make up for the suffering of all these people. No-one can and we can never understand – or forgive – only God can.

What happened in Denmark gives us hope. It must never be forgotten and neither must all those Danes, mostly unknown, who took part – to make this 'Light in the Darkness' possible.

My parents and I with the couple in whose cellar we were hiding, Copenhagen, 1943

The Future

After the War, when the Danish Jews were busy re-establishing themselves in Denmark, the fleeing and the traumas surrounding these events were best forgotten. People were told it was not good for them to dwell on these matters. Not that the Danish Jews were not grateful for their rescue – this was expressed repeatedly in special services and on anniversaries, and thanks were shown to the people who helped you personally by giving them presents and including them at family celebrations like birthdays, Barmitzvahs and weddings. How could you ever forget people who saved your life?

But whenever the subject of people's personal experiences and memories appeared, there was a deep silence – in our family at least. As a child this felt a very dangerous moment, because the adult faces changed, their voices became very emotional and one of my parents had to leave the room. I had so many questions I wanted to ask, but how could I ask, when it would make them cry? I would ask them about small practical matters, also how they withstood the humiliation, how they felt, and how brave they were.

The same happened in the Jewish school, Caroline Skolen. We never touched on the subject, and in my class we had all been three-year-olds hiding and fleeing as best we could during the October nights in 1943.

The understanding of trauma experiences has changed since those early years, but it took a long time before the survivors of the Holocaust were able to express their feelings. For some it came too late.

Soon the generation of survivors will be here no more, and it is vital that the second, third and fourth generation of families who went through these experiences continue telling the story to their children, so it will never be forgotten.

Tell the story with pride, how your family refused to become victims or dehumanised, how calm and brave they were, how they survived against all the odds – and how the love for their children came before everything else.

Above left: Anita and Philip
Above right: Nina and Jan
Left: Nina and Jonnie's wedding day, 1991
Below: Nina and Jonnie with Sam,
Rachel and Ben

*Right: Jan and Irene on their
wedding day, 1997
Below: Jan and Irene with Hannah,
Reuben and Sophie
Bottom: Anita with her
grandchildren (left to right):
Sam, Reuben, Sophie, Ben, Rachel
and Hannah*

Further Reading

Bertelsen, Aage, *Oktober 43*, Jydsk Central Trykkeris Forlag, Aarhus, 1952.

Foighel, Isi, *The Miracle in Denmark: The Rescue of the Jews*, Christian Ejlers, 2007.

Gilbert, Martin, *Final Journey: The Fate of the Jews in Nazi Europe*, George Allen & Unwin, London/ Boston/ Sydney, 1979.

Gilbert, Martin, *Auschwitz and the Allies*, Hamlyn Paperbacks, London, 1983.

Kreth, Rasmus, *Flugten Til Sverige (Escape to Sweden)*, Michael Mogensen, Gyldendal, 1967.

Melchior, Dr. Marcus, *A Rabbi Remembers*, Lyle Stuart, New York, 1965.

Morse, Arthur D, *While Six Million Died: A Chronicle of American Apathy*, Hart Publishing, New York City, 1968.

Neuman, Bertil, *En Miljon Bortglömda Hjältar (A Million Forgotten Heroes)*, Carlssons, 1999.

Oppenheim, Ralph, *Det Skulle så Være: Dagbog fra Theresienstadt (It Had to Be: Diary from Theresienstadt)*, Carit, 1966.

Schoenberner, Gerhard, *The Yellow Star*, Butler & Tanner, Frome and London, 1969.

Toksvig, Sandi, *Hitler's Canary*, Doubleday, London, 2005.

Acknowledgements

I would like to express my thanks especially to my husband, Philip, and my two children, Jan and Nina, for all the encouragement and support they have given me in the writing of this book. Thanks to my daughter-in-law, Irene, for doing the typing, and to my publisher, Helen Sandler, for all her help and her sensitive editing.

Anita Canter – May 2009